Te

by Kris Bonnell

A music teacher can teach us how to sing.

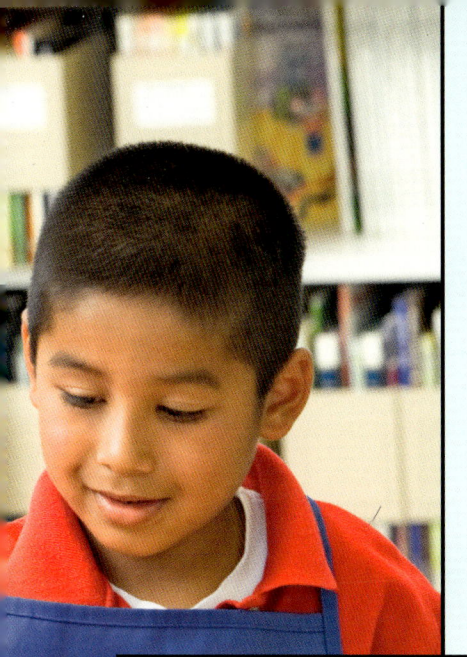

An art teacher can teach us how to paint.

A P.E. teacher can teach us how to play sports.

A computer teacher can teach us how to use a computer.

A math teacher can teach us how to add.

A reading teacher can teach us how to read.